The Kitchen At Grandma's House

The Kitchen At Grandma's House

DELLA WEST

ISBN-13: 9780692843178
ISBN-10: 0692843175

This book is dedicated to Lorene Elmgren. Thank you, Grandma, for leaving me the precious legacy of your old wooden recipe box.

Contents

One

SALADS AND DRESSINGS

Marshmallow Frozen Fruit Salad

20 marshmallows
2 medium oranges (about 1 cup), quartered sections
1 medium grapefruit (about 1 cup), quartered sections
3 pineapple slices (about 1 cup), diced
2 ripe bananas (about 1 2/3 cups), sliced
1 1/2 cups salad dressing

Cut marshmallows into eighths. Combine fruits and marshmallows and toss lightly. Add salad dressing. Pour into dishes and freeze for two to three hours. Cut into squares or oblongs; serve on a bed of crisp lettuce. Garnish with salted peanuts.

Servings: 12

Nellie T.'s Cottage Cheese and Pineapple Salad

1 package lemon Jell-O
1 package lime Jell-O
2 cups boiling water
1 cup walnuts, chopped
1 cup mayonnaise
1 lb. creamed cottage cheese
1 can grated pineapple, drained
2 tablespoons horseradish sauce

Mix the first three ingredients thoroughly, until they are the consistency of a syrup. Add in the rest of the ingredients, and stir to combine. Serve chilled.

Fall Salad

6 firm tomatoes
1 cup cucumber, diced
1/2 cup celery, diced
2 tablespoons onions, chopped
2 tablespoons chili sauce
2 tablespoons pickle relish
1/4 teaspoon salt

Wash and peel and remove seeds from the tomatoes. Chill. Mix and chill the rest of the ingredients. Stuff the tomatoes. Serve on lettuce. Serves 6.

Pineapple Cheese Salad

16 marshmallows
3/4 cup pineapple juice
1 cup crushed pineapple
1 pint cottage cheese
1 banana, crushed
3/4 cup whipped cream

Heat marshmallows and two tablespoons of pineapple juice in a saucepan over low heat Fold over and over until marshmallows are almost melted. Remove from the heat continue folding until mixture is smooth. Cool. Fold in remaining ingredients and freeze.

Servings: 8

Almond Salad

1/4 lb. almonds
12 marshmallows
12 candied cherries
6 almond macaroons
1 package strawberry Jell-O
1 pint boiling water
1 cup whipped cream
1/4 cup sugar

Finely chop the almonds, marshmallows, candied cherries, and almond macaroons. Combine and place into the refrigerator. Add the Jell-O to the water and stir until dissolved. Allow to cool. Mix ingredients when cold. Add in the whipped cream and sugar. Pour into pan and let harden. Serve with whipped cream and a cherry on top.

Perfection Salad

1 package lemon Jell-O
1 cup hot water
3/4 cup cold water
1/4 cup lemon juice or white vinegar
1/4 teaspoon salt
1 cup cabbage, shredded
1/2 cup celery, sliced
1/4 cup green peppers, chopped
1/4 cup pimientos, chopped
2 teaspoons onions, minced

Dissolve the gelatin in hot water. Add cold water, lemon juice, and salt. Chill until slightly thickened. Add the vegetables, and place in dishes. Chill until firm.

Surprise Pear Salad

8 canned pear halves
1 cup cottage cheese
1/4 cup nuts, chopped
1/4 cup mayonnaise
cherries and mayonnaise for garnish
lettuce leaves

Drain pear halves. Blend together the cottage cheese, chopped nuts, and mayonnaise. Spread four pear halves with the mixture. Press the remaining pear halves on top of the prepared ones, forming four whole pairs. Place each pear on a lettuce leaf, and garnish with mayonnaise and a cherry.

Servings: 4

Fruit Slaw

2 cups cabbage, chopped
1/2 cup marshmallows, diced
1/3 cup dates, diced
1/2 cup pineapple, diced
1/3 cup peaches, diced
1 teaspoon lemon juice
1/4 teaspoon salt
1/3 cup salad dressing

Chill ingredients. Combine, and serve in a bowl lined with crisp lettuce or any other salad green.

Vegetable Salad

1 package macaroni
1 can baked beans
1/2 medium head of cabbage, chopped
2 tablespoons celery seed
1 onion, diced
1 green pepper, cubed
4 hardboiled eggs
mayonnaise

Cook macaroni according to the directions on the package. Drain and chill. Drain beans. Dice two eggs. Combine the macaroni, vegetables, and diced eggs, and mix well. Add the celery seed, and season to taste. Mix with mayonnaise dressing. Slice two eggs for garnishing.

Peanut Oil French Dressing

2 teaspoons salt
1 teaspoon dry mustard
1 teaspoon paprika
2 teaspoons powdered sugar
1/2 cup white vinegar
1 1/3 cups peanut oil

Mix the salt, mustard, paprika, sugar, and vinegar together. Beat in the peanut oil. Shake thoroughly before using. Makes about one pint.

French Dressing

1 cup oil
1/2 cup catsup
1/2 cup white vinegar
1/3 onion, finely chopped
1 teaspoon paprika
1/3 green pepper, finely chopped
1 teaspoon salt
1/4 cup sugar
juice of 1 lemon

Combine all ingredients, and mix well.

Quick Change Dressing

1/2 teaspoon salt
1/4 teaspoon sugar
dash white pepper
1/2 teaspoon dry mustard
3/4 cup oil
1/4 cup white vinegar

Shake all ingredients in a jar for two minutes.

This recipe is a good dressing for general use. To change things up, try these variations.

Add 4 1/4 tablespoons India relish for tossed-greens salads.
Add 1/2 cup honey for fruit salads.
Add 1/2 cup tomato juice for seafood salads.

Two

Breads

Apple Toast

6 apples
6 tablespoons butter
6 tablespoons powdered sugar, to taste
2 tablespoons water
6 slices of bread

Peel, core, and quarter the apples. Cut them in slices and cook together with three tablespoons butter, powdered sugar, and water. Brown the slices of bread to a golden brown in three tablespoons butter. Place on a dish, cover with a little powdered sugar, top with the stewed apples, and serve hot.

Servings: 6

Scotch Scones

3 cups flour
1 teaspoon salt
1 teaspoon cream of tartar
2 teaspoons sugar
1 teaspoon baking soda
1 tablespoon butter, melted
buttermilk

Sift the flour with salt, sugar, cream of tartar, and baking soda. Add butter and sufficient buttermilk to make a soft dough. Cook in a frying pan or griddle, browning first one side and then the other.

Orange Biscuits

2 cups flour, sifted
4 teaspoons baking powder
1 tablespoon sugar
1/2 teaspoon salt
1/4 cup shortening
1/2 cup milk
12 sugar cubes
3 tablespoons orange juice
1 tablespoon preserved ginger syrup

Preheat oven to 450 degrees. Sift the dry ingredients together. Cut in short-ening thoroughly. Combine lightly with milk to make a soft, slightly moist dough. Do not overmix. Roll out on a lightly floured board to a thickness of 3/4 inch. Cut with a small biscuit cutter, and place in muffin tins. Combine the orange juice and ginger syrup. Working with one cube at a time, dip into the orange juice and ginger syrup mixture, and then press into the top of each biscuit. Bake for ten to twelve minutes. Serve decorated with a candied cherry half.

Servings: 12 biscuits

Apple Fritters

1 cup flour, sifted
1 1/2 teaspoons baking powder
1/4 cup sugar
1 1/4 teaspoons salt
1 egg, beaten
1/3 cup milk
1 tablespoon shortening, melted
2 large apples, peeled and sliced in eighths

Sift the flour, baking powder, sugar, and salt together. Combine the egg and milk; add to dry ingredients, beating until smooth. Add shortening and mix well.

Dip apples in batter and fry in shortening for about four minutes or until brown. Drain on paper towels. Serve with cinnamon sauce (recipe below).

Servings: 6

Cinnamon Sauce

1 cup sugar
1/4 teaspoon cinnamon
2 tablespoons flour
dash salt
2 cups boiling water
1 tablespoon butter
1 tablespoon lemon juice

Mix the sugar, cinnamon, flour, and salt in a saucepan. Add boiling water, stirring constantly until blended. Add the butter and boil for five minutes. Remove from the burner, add lemon juice, and serve hot.

Three

ENTREES AND SIDE DISHES

Escalloped Chicken with Mushrooms

6 tablespoons butter
8 tablespoons flour
2 cups milk
2 cups chicken stock
1/2 teaspoon salt
1/4 teaspoon paprika
2 tablespoons green peppers, diced and cooked
2 tablespoons pimientos, chopped
2 cups chicken, diced and cooked
1 cup mushrooms, browned

Melt the butter. Add the flour and blend. Add the milk and stock, and cook until creamy. Stirring constantly, add the rest of ingredients. Pour into a buttered baking dish and cover with crumbs (recipe below). Bake at 350 F. for twenty-five minutes.

Crumbs

3 tablespoons butter
2/3 cup bread crumbs

Mix ingredients.

Savory Noodles and Pork

1/4 lb. egg noodles (1 cup uncooked)
3/4 lb. pork butts, ground
2 small onions, chopped
2 cups celery, chopped
1 can tomato soup
1/3 cup water
3/4 cup grated cheese
1 teaspoon salt
1/8 teaspoon pepper

Preheat oven to 350 degrees. Cook noodles according to the directions on the package. Brown the meat. Add onions and celery, and cook for ten minutes. Add the cooked noodles. Measure the grated cheese by packing it into a measuring cup, and then add to the meat mixture. Add the tomato soup, water, salt, and pepper. Place in a buttered casserole dish and bake for forty-five minutes.

Servings: 6

Tuna and Noodle Casserole

1/2 lb. noodles (2 cups uncooked)
1 pound canned tuna
1/4 cup pimientos, chopped
2 cups canned peas, drained
salt and pepper
2 cups thin white sauce
buttered bread crumbs or Wheaties

Preheat oven to 350 degrees. Cook noodles according to the directions on the package. Place a layer of noodles on the bottom of a buttered baking dish, followed by layers of fish, pimiento, and peas. Season with salt and pepper. Repeat until all ingredients are used. Pour white sauce (recipe below) over the final layer. Sprinkle top with buttered bread crumbs or Wheaties. Bake for one hour.

Servings: 8

Thin White Sauce

2 tablespoons butter
2 tablespoons flour
1/2 teaspoon salt
1/8 teaspoon pepper
2 cups milk

Melt the butter in a saucepan. Blend in the flour and spices. Add the cold milk, stirring constantly. Remove from the burner for a few minutes and stir to prevent lumping. Return to stove and cook until thickened, stirring constantly. Cook for about ten minutes to eliminate the raw taste.

Swedish Meatballs

1/2 lb. lean pork, ground
1 lb. round steak, ground
1/2 cup onions, chopped
2 tablespoons butter
1 whole egg
1 egg yolk
1/2 cup bread crumbs
2 cups milk
salt and pepper

The pork and round steak should be ground very finely and mixed together. Cook the onion in the butter and cool. Beat together the egg and the egg yolk. Combine the meat, the onions, and the egg. Add the bread crumbs and milk, and season to taste. Chill the mixture in the refrigerator for an hour and a half. Form into small balls and fry.

Milk-Baked Ham

1 ham slice, 2 inches thick
milk
salt and pepper

Preheat oven to 375 degrees. Place the slice of ham in a baking dish, and completely cover it with milk. Bake until the ham is nicely browned. Serve on a platter, and garnish with browned potatoes.

Note: Gravy may be prepared by thickening the milk ham was baked in with a smooth blend of flour and water.

Ham Casserole

1 lb. ham-butt slices
1 cup canned corn
1 egg
1 cup bread crumbs, coarse
1 cup celery, chopped
1 onion, chopped
1/3 green pepper, chopped
1 cup milk
1/8 teaspoon pepper
4 tablespoons butter
1/2 teaspoon salt
2 tablespoons flour
1 cup buttered bread crumbs

Preheat oven to 325 degrees. Simmer ham in a small amount of water for ten minutes. Sauté the chopped onion, green pepper, and celery in two tablespoons of butter. Beat the egg, and add to the mixture, along with the corn, ½ cup buttered bread crumbs, salt, and pepper. Mix together. Place a slice of ham in a casserole dish; cover with the corn mixture and another slice of ham. Make white sauce by melting butter and adding flour and milk. Cook until thick, and pour over the top of casserole. Cover with ½ cup buttered bread crumbs. Bake for forty-five minutes.

Servings: 6

Pasta Ring of Plenty

3 cups cooked macaroni
2 cups cheese, diced
2 cups soft bread crumbs
2 tablespoons parsley, minced
1 small can pimientos, minced
6 tablespoons butter
2 tablespoons onion, minced
2 cups milk, scalded
2 eggs, well beaten
2 teaspoons salt
1/4 teaspoon pepper

Preheat oven to 350 degrees. Cook pasta according to the directions on the package. Combine with remaining ingredients. Pour into a buttered mold and steam bake. Remove from the mold and fill the center with meat, fish, or vegetables. Serve hot.

Clear Tomato Soup

2 cups water
2 teaspoons sugar
bay leaf
1 tablespoon onion, minced
1 1/2 teaspoons salt
1/8 teaspoon pepper
4 cups tomatoes, cooked
2 tablespoons butter
3 tablespoons flour

Add water, sugar, bay leaf, onion, salt, and pepper to the tomatoes. Cook for twenty minutes. Strain. Melt butter, blend with flour, and add strained tomatoes. Cook for five minutes.

Servings: 6

Fried Cornmeal Mush

9 cups water
2 teaspoons salt
3 cups yellow cornmeal
cracker crumbs, fine
cracker crumbs, coarse
1 egg, beaten
1 tablespoon milk

Measure water into a heavy pan and cover tightly. When boiling rapidly, add salt. While stirring, sift the cornmeal slowly into the pan to make the mush smooth. Cover tightly and let steam for twenty-five minutes to cook thoroughly and avoid a raw taste.

Pour into a square pan and refrigerate overnight. Cut into cubes. Roll in the fine cracker crumbs. Combine the beaten egg and the milk. Dip the cubes into the mixture, and then roll in the coarse cracker crumbs. Fry in deep fat, drain, and serve with maple syrup.

Leslie's Lima Bean Soufflé

1 cup dried lima beans, cooked
4 tablespoons butter
4 tablespoons flour
1 cup milk
3 eggs, separated
1/2 teaspoon salt
1 teaspoon onion, minced
pepper

Preheat oven to 350 degrees. Rub lima beans through a coarse strainer. Make white sauce of butter, flour, and milk. Add lima beans, egg yolks, and spices. Mix well, and set aside. Beat the egg whites. Fold the lime beans mixture into the beaten egg whites. Pour into a buttered casserole dish and bake for about thirty minutes. Serve plain or with tomato sauce.

Glazed Squash

1 Hubbard squash
glazing syrup

Preheat oven to 350 degrees. Cut the squash into three- to four-inch pieces. Peel and parboil until partially tender. Drain and place into a shallow baking pan. Pour glazing syrup (recipe below) over the squash pieces. Bake for about thirty minutes, until tender, basting frequently with the syrup.

Glazing Syrup

1/2 cup sugar
1/2 cup brown sugar
1/2 cup water
2 tablespoons butter

Combine the sugars and water together and cook just until blended. Add the butter.

Four

DESSERTS

Lady Betty Cake

2/3 cup butter
1 1/2 cups sugar
4 eggs, separated
1 2/3 cup flour
1/4 teaspoon salt
2 teaspoons baking powder
1 cup milk
3 squares baking chocolate, melted
1 cup nuts, chopped

Preheat oven to 325 degrees. Cream butter thoroughly. Add the sugar and mix well. Add the egg yolks and mix well. Set aside. Beat the egg whites. Set aside. Sift together the flour, salt, and baking powder. Add the nuts. Add the flour mixture and milk alternately and a little at a time to the egg mixture. Mix thoroughly. Add the melted chocolate just before the last of flour. Fold in the beaten egg whites. Pour into a well-greased and floured nine-inch tube pan. Bake for an hour and fifteen minutes; turn out and cool.

White Nut Cake

1/2 cup shortening
1 cup sugar
2/3 cup milk
2 cups pastry flour
3 teaspoons baking powder
1/2 teaspoon salt
1/2 cup walnuts, finely chopped
1 teaspoon vanilla extract
3 egg whites, stiffly beaten

Preheat oven to 375 degrees. Cream together the shortening and sugar. Set aside. Sift the flour, baking powder, and salt together. Add alternately with the milk to the sugar mixture. Beat well. Add the nuts and vanilla. Fold in the stiffly beaten egg whites. Bake for thirty minutes.

Cream Spice Cake

2 cups brown sugar
1/2 cup shortening
3 egg yolks
3 egg whites, stiffly beaten
2 teaspoons ground cloves
2 teaspoons cinnamon
2 teaspoons allspice
1 cup sour cream
2 cups pastry flour
1/4 teaspoon salt
1 teaspoon baking soda

Preheat oven to 375 degrees. Cream together the sugar and shortening until thoroughly blended. Add the beaten egg yolk, cinnamon, cloves, and allspice, and beat well. Set aside. Sift together the flour, salt, and baking soda. Add to the sugar mixture alternately with the sour cream. Fold in the stiffly beaten egg whites. Bake for thirty minutes.

Cherry Checkerboard

2 1/4 cups flour
1 tablespoon baking powder
1/2 teaspoon salt
1 1/4 cup + 2 tablespoons sugar, divided
5 tablespoons butter
3/4 cup milk
2 cups sour red cherries, pitted and drained
1/2 cup water

Preheat oven to 350 degrees. Sift the flour, baking powder, salt, and sugar together. Cut in the butter. Make a well in the center of the flour mixture; add milk. Mix with a fork. Turn out dough onto floured board and knead lightly for a few seconds. Roll dough into a nine-inch by twelve-inch rectangle. Spread cherries over dough, and sprinkle with 3/4 cup of sugar. Roll as for a jelly roll, starting from the long side. Cut into nine pieces.

Boil water and 1/2 cup sugar to make a medium-thick syrup. Pour hot syrup into well-greased square baking pan. Place pieces of rolled dough on top of syrup, cut side up. Bake for about thirty minutes. Serve with hot cherry sauce (recipe below).

Cherry Sauce

1/4 cup sugar
3 tablespoons flour
1 cup cherry juice
1 tablespoon butter

Combine the sugar and the flour. Slowly add the cherry juice. Stir and cook until smooth and thick. Add one tablespoon butter.

Deep South Pecan Wafers

2 cups flour, sifted
1/4 teaspoon salt
1/2 cup shortening
1 cup sugar
1 egg yolk, unbeaten
1 egg white, unbeaten
2 tablespoons milk
1 teaspoon vanilla
1 cup pecans, finely chopped

Preheat oven to 350 degrees. Sift the flour once and measure. Add salt and sift again. Set aside. Cream shortening. Add sugar gradually, creaming well. Add egg yolk and beat thoroughly. Add milk, vanilla, and dry ingredients. Mix well. Roll 1/8 inch thick on lightly floured board. Brush with egg white and cut into squares of 1 1/2 inches by 1 1/2 inches. Sprinkle with pecans. Bake on greased baking sheet for about fifteen minutes.

Chews

1 cup dates, chopped
1 cup pecans, chopped
1 cup sugar
3/4 cup flour
2 eggs
1 teaspoon baking powder
1/4 teaspoon salt

Preheat oven to 325 degrees. Beat eggs and add to sugar. Set aside. Sift the flour, salt, and baking powder over dates and nuts. Add sugar mixture to flour, nuts, and dates; stir to combine. Spread mixture into greased pans, and bake for about forty minutes.

Canteen Cookies

1/2 cup shortening
3/4 teaspoon salt
1 tablespoon orange rind, grated
2 tablespoons orange juice
1 cup brown sugar, firmly packed
2 eggs
2 cups flour, sifted
1 teaspoon baking powder
1/4 teaspoon baking soda
1/2 cup nuts, chopped
8 ounces chocolate chips

Preheat oven to 375 degrees. Blend the shortening, salt, orange rind, and juice. Add brown sugar gradually and cream well. Add eggs one at a time, beating well after each addition. Sift the flour with baking powder and baking soda. Add to the creamed mixture and mix thoroughly. Add nuts and chocolate. Blend. Drop from tablespoon on greased baking sheet and bake for ten to twelve minutes.

Servings: 3 1/2 dozen cookies

Marshmallow Dessert

1/2 lb. marshmallows
1/2 cup milk
1/2 pint whipping cream
12 graham crackers

In a double boiler, melt the marshmallows and milk. Cool. Fold in the whipping cream. Place half of the graham crackers in the bottom of a dish, and pour the mixture over them. Add the remainder of the graham crackers on top. Chill in the refrigerator at least two hours.

www.ingramcontent.com/pod-product-compliance
Lightning Source LLC
Chambersburg PA
CBHW060629030426
42337CB00018B/3278